DATE DUE

GREAT AMERICAN SHORT STORIES

Edgar Allan Poe

Stories retold by Emily Hutchinson

Illustrated by James McConnell

GARETH**STEVENS**
PUBLISHING
A World Almanac Education Group Company

Please visit our web site at: www.garethstevens.com
For a free color catalog describing Gareth Stevens Publishing's
list of high-quality books and multimedia programs, call
1-800-542-2595 (USA) or 1-800-387-3178 (Canada).
Gareth Stevens Publishing's fax: (414) 332-3567.

Library of Congress Cataloging-in-Publication Data

Hutchinson, Emily.
    Edgar Allan Poe / stories retold by Emily Hutchinson; illustrated by James McConnell.
        p. cm. — (Great American short stories)
        Summary: Adaptations of four tales of horror and the supernatural by Edgar Allan Poe,
    plus an introduction to the author and discussion questions.
        Contents: The cask of amontillado—The masque of the Red Death—The tell-tale heart—
    The black cat.
        ISBN 0-8368-4254-5 (lib. bdg.)
        1. Children's stories, American. 2. Horror tales, American. [1. Supernatural—Fiction.
    2. Horror stories. 3. Short stories.] I. Poe, Edgar Allan, 1809–1849. II. McConnell,
    James, ill. III. Title. IV. Series.
    PZ7.H961657Ed   2004
    [Fic]—dc22   2004045210

This North American hardcover edition published in 2005 with the
permission of AGS Publishing exclusively by
Gareth Stevens Publishing
A World Almanac Education Group Company
330 West Olive Street, Suite 100
Milwaukee, WI 53212 USA

Copyright © 2005 by AGS Publishing. Original edition copyright © 1994
AGS Publishing, 4201 Woodland Road, Circle Pines, MN 55014-1796,
1-800-328-2560, www.agsnet.com. AGS Publishing is a trademark and
trade name of American Guidance Service, Inc.

Gareth Stevens editor: Barbara Kiely Miller
Gareth Stevens cover and text design: Steve Schraenkler
Gareth Stevens picture researcher: Diane Laska-Swanke

Cover Photo: © Hulton Archive/Getty Images

Printed in the United States of America

1 2 3 4 5 6 7 8 9 08 07 06 05 04

CONTENTS

Introduction

*"The universe is made of
stories, not atoms."*
— Muriel Rukeyser

"The story's about you."
— Horace

Everyone loves a good story. It is hard
to think of a friendlier introduction to
classic literature. For one thing, short
stories are *short*—quick to get into and
easy to finish. Of all the literary forms,
the short story is the least intimidating
and the most approachable.

Great literature is an important part of
our human heritage. In the belief that
this heritage belongs to everyone, the
Great American Short Stories series is
adapted for today's readers. Lengthy
sentences and paragraphs are shortened.
Archaic words are replaced. Modern
punctuation and spellings are used. Many
of the longer stories are abridged. In all
the stories, painstaking care has been

taken to preserve the author's unique voice.

Great American Short Stories has something for everyone. The stories in the collection cover a broad terrain of themes, story types, and styles. Literary merit was a deciding factor in story selection. No story was included, however, unless it was as enjoyable as it was instructive. And special priority was given to stories that shine light on the human condition.

Each book in the *Great American Short Stories* series is devoted to the work of a single author. Little-known stories of merit are included with famous, old favorites. Taken as a whole, the collected authors and stories make up a rich and diverse sampler of the storyteller's art.

Great American Short Stories guarantees a great reading experience. Readers who look for common interests, concerns, and experiences are sure to find them. Readers who bring their own gifts of perception and appreciation to the stories will be doubly rewarded.

❧ Edgar Allan Poe ❧
(1809—1849)

About the Author

The life of Edgar Allan Poe was as tormented as his stories. His parents were traveling actors who died before he was two years old. His wealthy guardian disinherited him. He was expelled from the University of Virginia and West Point because of gambling debts and heavy drinking. His teenaged bride, a cousin, died of tuberculosis in her early twenties.

When it came to his writing, however, Poe was a great talent and an extremely hard worker. He wrote poetry, short stories, and literary criticism. His tales of mystery, horror, and crime laid the basis for the modern detective story. Few writers have ever come close to achieving Poe's dramatic power and emotional intensity.

In a very real way, Edgar Allan Poe is the architect of the modern short story.

In 1832, he was the first to insist that the short story should be built around a single effect. Another of his ideas had to do with a story's length. He believed that a reader should be able to finish a story "in a single sitting."

Poe did not create the short story as a literary form, but he was the first to create the "science" of the short story by formulating its rules.

Poe is widely regarded as one of the most important American authors of the nineteenth century. He is remembered for his poetry as well as for his popular tales of horror. If thrills and chills are what you want from a story, Edgar Allan Poe has just what you're looking for.

The Cask of Amontillado

How far would you go to get revenge for an insult? In this strange tale, you will meet two wealthy men who appreciate fine wine. One man is vain but foolish. The other is clever but evil. The combination could be deadly.

THERE IS NO JOY IN GETTING REVENGE IF YOU
YOURSELF ARE PUNISHED FOR IT LATER.

The Cask of Amontillado

Fortunato had offended me thousands of times, and I put up with it as well as I could. But when he insulted me, I vowed I would get even with him. Of course, I did not say anything about this to Fortunato. I knew that I would have my revenge, no matter how long it took.

Because I was in no hurry, I could make my plan carefully. There was no chance of any risk to me. Not only would I punish Fortunato, but I would punish him without any danger to myself. There is no joy in getting revenge if you yourself are punished for it later. There is also no joy in it unless you make sure your enemy knows what you are doing.

You must understand that I never said or did anything to let Fortunato know what I was thinking of. He had no doubt that I was his good friend. I continued, as was my habit, to smile in his face. He did not suspect that I was only smiling at the thought of my revenge.

In almost everything, Fortunato was a man to be respected and even feared. But he had a weak point. Fortunato was very proud of his knowledge of wine. This was one thing we had in common—we both knew a lot about fine wines. I bought many bottles of good wine as often as I could. Then I stored my treasures in the vaults beneath my home. There, along with the bones of my ancestors, the wine could keep cool.

It was about dusk, one evening during the carnival season, that I ran into Fortunato. He greeted me warmly, for he had been enjoying the carnival. He wore brightly colored party clothes, including a hat with bells on it. I was so pleased to see him that I shook his hand for a long time.

I said, "My dear Fortunato, I'm so glad to see you. You look wonderful! Listen, I have just bought a cask full of wine. The seller tells me it is a fine amontillado, but I have my doubts."

"How did you get it? It's hard to find such a fine wine during the middle of the carnival!" said Fortunato.

"Well, I'm not so sure it's really amontillado. I was silly enough to pay the full price without asking you to sample it for me first. I couldn't find you anywhere, and I was afraid I'd miss a bargain."

"Amontillado!" said Fortunato.

"I have my doubts," I said.

"Amontillado!"

"And I must be sure about this," I said.

"Amontillado!" he said again.

"I see you are busy. I am on my way to visit Luchesi. He knows a lot about wine. Maybe he can help me," I said.

"Luchesi can't tell the difference between amontillado and ordinary sherry," said Fortunato.

"Yet some fools will say that Luchesi's taste in wines is as good as yours," I said.

"Come, let us go," said Fortunato.

"Where?"

"To your vaults, of course," said Fortunato.

"My friend, no. I can see that you are busy. I would not want to bother you. Luchesi—" I said.

"It is no bother. Let's go."

"My friend, no. I can see that you are suffering from a cold. My vaults are terribly damp. It wouldn't be good for you right now."

"Let us go anyway. The cold is nothing. Amontillado! As for Luchesi, he knows nothing about fine wines. As I said before, he cannot tell the difference between an ordinary sherry and an amontillado."

As he spoke, Fortunato took my arm. I let him lead the way to my home. All the servants were gone. They were all out enjoying the carnival. I had told them that I wouldn't be back until the morning. Then I had ordered them to stay inside the house. I knew that this order would be completely ignored. As soon as my back was turned, I was sure that they would all go to the carnival. So Fortunato and I were alone in the house, with no chance of being disturbed.

I led him through many rooms to the archway that opened to the vaults. We took lighted torches so we could see where we were going. I told him to be careful as we went down the long and winding staircase. Finally, we came to the bottom of the stairs. We stood together on the damp ground of the catacombs of the Montresors. It was the burial place of my family.

My friend was a little unsteady on his feet. The bells on his hat jingled as he walked.

"Where is the cask of amontillado?"

"It is farther on," I said. Just then, Fortunato began to cough. He coughed for several minutes.

"Come," I said. "We will go back. Your health is too precious. You are rich, respected, admired, and loved. You are a happy man, as I once was. You are a man who would be missed. For me, it does not matter. We will go back now. Otherwise, you will get ill, and I do not want to be responsible. Besides, there is always Luchesi—"

"Enough," he said. "The cough is nothing. It will not kill me. I shall not die of a cough."

"True, true," I said. "Indeed, I didn't mean to worry you, but you should be more careful about your health. A drink of this red wine will protect us from the dampness down here." I chose a bottle from a long row of them along the wall.

"Drink," I said, handing him the bottle.

He raised it to his lips. For a moment he stopped and nodded to me. The bells on his hat jingled.

"I drink," he said, "to those who are buried here and rest in these vaults."

"And I drink to your long life," I said.

He took my arm again, and we continued our walk.

"These burial chambers take up a lot of

space," he said.

"The Montresors were a great and large family," I replied.

"I have forgotten what your family's coat of arms looks like," Fortunato said.

"It is a large human foot made of gold, on a blue background. The foot is crushing a snake whose fangs are digging into the heel."

"And what words appear on the coat of arms?" asked Fortunato.

"No one injures me without being punished," I replied.

"Good!" he said.

The wine sparkled in his eyes, and the bells jingled. We had passed by walls where human bones were piled up. Casks and bottles of wine were stored here and there. We continued our walk, into the innermost places of the catacombs. Then I stopped again, but this time I grabbed Fortunato's arm above the elbow.

"We are below the river's bed now. See how the drops of moisture trickle among the bones. Come, we will go back before it is too late. Your cough—"

"It is nothing," he said. "Let us go on. But first, let us sample some more red wine."

I opened another bottle. He drank from it, and his eyes flashed with a fierce light. He laughed and threw the bottle upward with a gesture I did not understand.

I looked at him in surprise. He repeated the strange gesture.

"You do not understand?" he asked.

"No, I don't," I replied.

"Then you do not belong to the brotherhood."

"Pardon me?" I said.

"You are not one of the Masons," he said. Until then, I did not know that Fortunato was a member of this secret group.

"Yes, yes, I am," I said.

"You? Impossible! You could not be a Mason," he said.

"But I am," I insisted.

"Show me a sign," he said.

"Here it is," I answered, taking out a trowel from the folds of my cloak. This tool, used to spread mortar and cement, was a part of my plan.

"You are joking!" said Fortunato, backing up a few steps. "But let us go on to the amontillado."

"All right," I said, replacing the tool beneath my cloak. I offered him my arm, and he leaned on it heavily. We continued our walk, passing through several low arches. We went deeper and deeper into the catacombs and finally arrived at a deep vault. The air in this chamber had a foul, stale odor. At the farthest end of this room was an opening into another, smaller room. Three of its walls were lined with human bones, which were piled high. The bones had been thrown down from the fourth wall, however. These bones lay in a pile on the floor. The fourth wall opened into yet another room, even smaller than the others. It was about four feet deep, three feet wide, and six or seven feet high. The tiny room seemed to have been built for no special reason. It just took up the space between two of the beams that supported the catacombs' ceiling. The back wall of this space was made of solid stone.

Fortunato lifted his lighted torch, trying to see into this small chamber. But the light was not strong enough to let him see to the back of the room.

"Go in," I said. "The amontillado is in there. As for Luchesi—"

"Luchesi is a fool," said Fortunato, as he stepped forward. I followed right behind him. In an instant, he had reached the back wall of the room. When he found that he could go no farther, he stood there, puzzled.

A moment later, I had him chained to the wall. The wall had two iron rings attached to it, about two feet apart. A short chain hung from one of these rings. A lock was attached to the other one. Throwing the chain around his waist, I quickly locked it onto the other ring. Fortunato was much too surprised to fight back. Taking the key from the lock, I stepped back.

"Pass your hand over the wall," I said. "You will notice that it is very damp. Once more, let me beg you to return.

No? Then I must leave you here. But I must first give you all the little attentions in my power."

"The amontillado!" he cried, still thinking I meant to have him sample the wine. He had not yet recovered from his surprise.

"True," I replied. "The amontillado."

As I said these words, I turned toward the pile of bones on the floor. Throwing the bones aside, I soon uncovered a stack of building stones and mortar. Using my trowel, I started to build a wall in front of Fortunato.

I had hardly finished laying the first row of stones when I noticed that Fortunato was beginning to sober up. The first clue I had was a low moaning cry. It was not the cry of a drunken man. After that, there was a long silence. I laid the second, third, and fourth rows. Then I heard the rattling of the chain. The noise lasted for several minutes. To better enjoy the sound, I stopped laying stones and sat down on the pile of bones.

When at last the noise stopped, I picked up the trowel again. I laid the fifth, the sixth, and the seventh layers of stones. The wall was now almost as tall as my chest. Again I stopped, and I held my torch up over the wall so I could see the figure within.

At once, Fortunato let forth a series of loud and terrible screams. These shrill screams burst forth so suddenly from his throat that the noise seemed to push me violently back. For a moment I didn't know what to do. I was trembling. Then I came closer to the wall and screamed back at Fortunato. Every time he screamed, I screamed louder. This went on for some time, and then he grew quiet.

It was now midnight, and my task was drawing to a close. I had completed the eighth, the ninth, and the tenth layers. I was almost finished with the last row, the eleventh one. There was room for only one more stone. I struggled with the weight of the last stone and placed it partly in position. Then I heard a low laugh that caused the hairs on my head to stand up. After that, I heard a sad voice, which I could hardly recognize as belonging to the proud and noble Fortunato.

The voice said "Ha! ha! ha! hee! hee! A very good joke indeed—an excellent joke. We will have many a rich laugh about it later—over a glass of wine. Hee! hee! hee!"

"Over a glass of amontillado!" I said.

"Ha! ha! Yes, the amontillado. But is it not getting late? Won't someone be waiting for us at your house? Let us be gone."

"Yes," I said. "Let us be gone."

"For the love of God, Montresor!"

"Yes," I said. "For the love of God."

I listened for a reply, but there was none. I grew impatient.

I called aloud, "Fortunato!"

Still there was no answer. I pushed my torch through the remaining hole and let it fall inside. All I heard was the jingling of the bells. My heart grew sick—because of the dampness of the catacombs. I hurried to finish the wall. I forced the last stone into its position. And then I plastered it up. Finally, I piled up all the old bones against the new wall. For the last half a century no one has disturbed them. Rest in peace!

The Masque of the Red Death

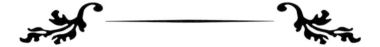

Can wealth and power prevent all bad fortune? In this story, a clever prince tries to save himself and his friends from a terrible plague. Will his plan work? Or will the deadly disease catch up with them?

THE CLEVER PRINCE HAD A PLAN TO ESCAPE FROM
THE DEADLY DISEASE.

The Masque of the Red Death

The "Red Death" had been terrorizing the country for months and months. The sickness was named after the color of blood. No disease had ever been so deadly or so horrible. First, its victims felt sharp pains and sudden dizziness. Then they began to bleed heavily from the pores of their skin. Death followed soon after. The red stains on their faces caused other people to stay away from them. The whole progress of the illness took only half an hour from start to finish.

Half the people of Prince Prospero's kingdom had died from the Red Death.

But Prince Prospero was not afraid. The clever prince had a plan to escape from the disease. He asked a thousand healthy and cheerful knights and ladies of his court to go away with him. Together, they went to one of his huge castles out in the country. This was a beautiful and magnificent building, designed by the prince himself. A strong, tall wall surrounded it. The wall had iron gates. After the people had all gone inside, the locks and bolts on the gates were welded together. No one else would be allowed to enter, and those inside would not be allowed to leave.

Everyone in the castle had plenty to eat and drink. The prince had made sure that they could hold out until the disease had run its course. The rest of the world would have to take care of itself. In the meantime, it was foolish to be sad or even to think. The prince had provided everything to make sure his guests had a good time. There were clowns, actors, dancers, and musicians. And best of all, there was safety within the castle walls.

Outside was the Red Death.

Five or six months passed. Outside the castle walls, the disease was getting even worse. But inside the walls, Prince Prospero was preparing to entertain his friends at a masked ball. The grand party would be held in the castle's most elegant suite of rooms.

There were seven large rooms in the suite. Every twenty or thirty yards, there was a sharp turn from one room to the next. With each turn, the room became entirely different. To the right and left, in the middle of each wall, was a tall and narrow window. Each window looked out on a twisting hallway that led nowhere. These windows were of stained glass. The color of the glass matched the color of everything else in the room. For example, the window on the east side was blue— just like the drapes, carpets, and furniture in the room. The second room had purple furniture and wall hangings —and here the window glass was purple. The third room was green throughout, and so were the windows. The fourth was furnished and lighted with orange. The fifth was all white, and the sixth was violet. The seventh room had black velvet hung all over the ceiling and down the walls. The drapes fell in heavy folds upon a carpet of black velvet. But in this room only, the color of the windows did not match the decorations. The window panes here were red—a deep blood color.

None of the seven rooms had any lamps or candles. But just outside each window, in the twisting hallways, a pan of fire stood on a heavy table. The light from these fires lit up the rooms. Because of all the different colors of glass, the firelight made a fantastic and strange effect. But in the black room, the effect of the firelight was truly ghastly. The face of anyone who entered there was covered in a deathly, blood-tinted light. Very few of the guests were bold enough to set foot inside that room.

A gigantic clock made of ebony, a rich black wood, was also in the black room.Its pendulum swung back and forth with a dull and heavy sound. Every hour, the clock's chime rang out. The loud sound was clear, deep, and musical. It was also such a strange note that the musicians and dancers stopped what they were doing to listen. While those strange chimes were sounding, even the happiest people at the party grew pale.

Some guests passed their hands over their brows as if they were confused. But when the chiming sound ended, the guests began laughing again. The musicians looked at one another and smiled. They promised that the next chiming of the clock would not have such an effect on them. They promised that next time they would just keep on playing. But each hour, when the clock chimed, everyone fell silent again. It was as if they couldn't help it.

In spite of all this, it was a wonderful party. The prince had gone to a lot of trouble to make sure that everyone was entertained. The different colors of decorations in the seven rooms were all his idea. He had given his guests their choice of amazing costumes. The costumes were of all types. Some were quite grotesque, and others were quite beautiful. Some were strange, and others were frightening. Some could even be called disgusting.

Laughing and talking, the guests wandered in and out of the seven rooms. As they moved, they took on the colors of the various rooms, as reflected in the firelight. The wild music of the orchestra seemed to echo their steps. And on and on, through the night, the ebony clock struck each hour. Each time, all was still and all was silent except the voice of the clock. Then the echoes of the chime died away, and a light laughter began again.

As the night wore on, none of the guests dared to enter the black room. But all the other rooms were crowded, and the party went on. At last the ebony clock struck midnight. As the chiming began, all the music and dancing stopped. As before, all the talking and laughing stopped, too. But this time, there were twelve strokes to be sounded by the bell of the clock. Before the last chime had faded, many people in the crowd noticed a stranger. Before this, no one had been aware of this masked figure. A buzz, a murmur, arose from the crowd. This buzz soon turned into an expression of terror, of horror, and of disgust.

In any ordinary masked ball, of course, a frightening costume would not have caused such a reaction. It was certainly true that many of the other costumes were terrifying, horrifying, disgusting. But this strange, new figure had gone beyond the limits of the acceptable. Even to people who joke about life and death, there are matters of which no joke can be made. Suddenly, everyone at once seemed to feel deeply that the stranger's costume was neither funny nor proper.

The figure was tall and thin. It was covered from head to foot in the wrappings of the grave. The mask that hid the face looked just like the face of a corpse. Even that might have been acceptable to the guests, except for one thing. The costumed figure had gone so far as to dress up like a victim of the Red

Death. Its clothing was covered in blood. And all the features of its face were sprinkled with the tell-tale red horror.

When the eyes of Prince Prospero fell on this ghostly image, he shuddered. This shudder was either because of terror or distaste—no one could be sure. But in the next moment, the prince's face became red with anger.

"Who dares to do such a thing?" he demanded. "Seize him and take off his mask! Then we shall know whom we must hang, at sunrise, from the castle walls!"

As he said these words, Prince Prospero was standing in the blue room. His words rang loudly and clearly through all the other rooms. This was because the prince had a bold, strong voice, and also because all the music had stopped.

At first, after the prince spoke, several men started to rush toward the stranger. But at that very moment, the stranger moved closer to the prince. The whole party felt a nameless fear of the stranger. Nobody put forth a hand to stop him. Soon he was within a yard of the prince.

At the same time, the guests, as if they were one, shrank back against the walls. The stranger made his way without interruption from the blue room to the purple one. Then he moved from the purple to the green, and then to the orange. From there, he went to the white, and then to the violet. Still, no movement had been made to stop him. The guests seemed frozen in place.

It was then, however, that Prince Prospero became angry and ashamed of his own fears. He rushed quickly through the six rooms. No one followed him, because somehow everyone had been overcome with a deadly terror. The prince pulled out a dagger as he approached the stranger. When the masked figure reached the black room, it suddenly turned and faced the prince. Immediately, the prince made a sharp cry—and dropped the dagger on the black carpet. Then Prince Prospero himself fell to the carpet, dead.

Next, calling on the wild courage of despair, a group of guests ran into the black room. They seized the thin figure standing tall and still within the shadow of the ebony clock. As they grabbed at the clothing and the corpse-like mask, the guests gasped in horror. They found that there was nothing inside the costume!

Now they knew that the Red Death itself had arrived. He had come like a thief in the night. One by one he dropped the guests in the bloody halls of the castle. Each died in a desperate fall. And the life of the ebony clock went out with that of the last guest. And the flames of the fires died. And Darkness and Decay and the Red Death held supreme power over all.

The Tell-Tale Heart

What would you see if you looked into the mind of a madman? The main character in this story thinks clearly enough to plan a "perfect" murder. How can he be insane? The slowly building terror in this short tale has made it one of Poe's most famous stories.

A SINGLE DIM RAY, LIKE THE THREAD OF A SPIDER,
SHOT OUT AND FELL ON THE VULTURE EYE.

The Tell-Tale Heart

True! I had been and still am very nervous—very, very dreadfully nervous. But why will you say that I am mad? The disease had made my senses sharper. It had not destroyed or dulled them. Above all, my sense of hearing was sharp. I heard all things in the heaven and in the earth. How, then, can you say I am mad? Listen! You shall see how healthy and calm I am as I tell you the whole story.

It is impossible to say how I first got the idea. But once I had the thought, it haunted me day and night. There was no good reason for it. I didn't hate the old man. I loved him. He had never done anything against me. And he had never insulted me. I had no wish at all to take his gold.

I think it was his eye. Yes, that's what it was. One of his eyes looked like a vulture's eye. It was a pale blue eye, with a film over it. Whenever he looked at me, my blood ran cold. And so bit by bit, very slowly, I made up my mind to take the life of the old man. That way, I would rid myself of the eye forever.

Now this is the point. You think I am mad. But a person who is mad knows nothing. You should have seen *me* and how wisely I acted. I was cautious, and I planned ahead. I never gave the old man any reason to suspect. In fact, I was never kinder to him than during the whole week before I killed him.

Every night, about midnight, I turned the handle of his door and opened it— oh, so gently! When I had opened it just wide enough, I pushed a dark lantern through the crack. The lantern was covered, so that no light shone from it. Then I put my head in the door opening.

Oh, you would have laughed to see how I did it! I moved slowly—very, very slowly, so that I would not disturb the old man's sleep. It took me an hour to put my whole head inside the opening far enough so I could see the old man. Ha! Would someone who is mad have been this smart? And then, when my head was well in the room, I uncovered the lantern. I did this very cautiously, for the hinges creaked. I uncovered it just enough so that a single long ray of light fell upon the vulture eye.

I did this for seven long nights, every night just at midnight. But I found the eye was always closed. That made it impossible to do the work. You see, it was not the old man who upset me, but his Evil Eye. Every morning, when the day broke, I went boldly into his room, calling him by name in a friendly voice. I asked him how he had passed the night. I knew he had no idea that every night, just at midnight, I looked in upon him while he slept.

On the eighth night, I was more cautious than usual. A watch's minute hand moves more quickly than my hand did. Never before that night had I felt just how powerful and wise I really was. I could hardly control my feelings of triumph. There I was, opening the door, little by little. I knew that the old man couldn't even dream of my secret actions or thoughts. The very idea just about made me laugh out loud.

Perhaps he heard me, for he moved on the bed suddenly. It was as if he were surprised by something. Now you may think that I moved back, but I did not. The room was as black as tar, for the window shutters were closed tight. I knew that he could not see the opening of the door. So I kept pushing on it— slowly, slowly.

I had my head inside, and was about to uncover the lantern, when my thumb slipped. This small noise caused the old man to sit up in bed. I heard him cry out, "Who's there?" but I kept quite still and said nothing. For a whole hour, I did not move a muscle. In the meantime, I did not hear him lie down. He was still sitting up in the bed, listening.

After a time, I heard a slight groan. I knew it was a groan of deathly terror. It was not a groan of pain or of sorrow. Oh, no! It was the low sound that comes from the bottom of the soul when it is filled with dread. I knew the sound well. Many a night, just at midnight, I have made such a sound myself. As I did so, that very sound made my terrors even worse. Oh, yes, I knew that sound well.

I knew what the old man felt and I pitied him—even though I was laughing in my heart. I knew that he had been lying awake since the first slight noise. His fears had been growing ever since he had turned in the bed. He had been trying to talk himself out of being afraid, but he could not. He had been saying to himself, "It is nothing but the wind in the chimney. It is nothing but a mouse crossing the floor. It is only a cricket that has made a single chirp."

Yes, I knew very well that he had been trying to talk himself out of being afraid. But it wasn't working. Death, in coming near him, had cast its black shadow before him. Now the victim was surrounded. It was the unseen shadow of Death that made the old man feel my closeness. He could neither see nor hear me, but he could feel the presence of my head in that room.

After waiting a long time, I decided to open the lantern a tiny bit. You cannot imagine how carefully I did so. Finally, a single dim ray, like the thread of a spider, shot out and fell upon the vulture eye.

The eye was open—wide, wide open. I grew very angry as I looked at it. I saw it with perfect clearness. It was all a dull blue, with an ugly film over it. The sight of it chilled my very bones. I could see nothing else of the old man's face. The ray of light was pointing right at his eye.

Didn't I already tell you that what you think is madness is only a sharpness in my senses? Now, I say, I started to hear a low, dull, quick sound. It sounded like a watch wrapped in cotton. I knew *that* sound well, too. It was the beating of the old man's heart. Somehow that sound made me even angrier—just as the beating of a drum makes a soldier feel brave.

But even then I kept still. I hardly even breathed. I tried to see how steadily I could keep the lantern's ray shining on the eye. I heard the beating of the heart increase. It grew quicker and quicker, and louder and louder with every beat. The old man's terror *must* have been growing by the minute. His heartbeat grew louder, I say, louder every moment! Do you hear me?

I have told you that I am nervous. It is true. And now, in the awful silence of that old house, this noise terrifies me. Yet, for some minutes longer, I stood still. But the beating of the heart grew louder, louder! His heart sounded as if it might burst. Suddenly a new terror came upon me. I thought that the sound would be heard by a neighbor!

The old man's hour had come! With a

loud yell, I opened the lantern and leaped into the room. He screamed once—once only. In an instant, I dragged him to the floor and pulled the heavy bed over him. Then I smiled, to find the deed so close to being done. But, for many minutes, the heart beat on with a muffled sound. This, however, did not bother me. Under the heavy bed, the sound would not be heard through the wall.

Finally it stopped. The old man was dead. I moved the bed and looked at the body. Yes, he was stone, stone dead. I placed my hand on his heart and held it there for a few minutes. There was no beating. He was stone dead. That horrible eye would bother me no more.

If you still think I am mad, you will no longer think so when I tell you what I did next. I thought about the best way to hide the body. Then I cut it into pieces. I cut off the head and the arms and the legs.

Next I took up three boards from the floor of the bedroom. I put the body under the floor, and then put the boards back in place. I did this so well that no human eye—not even his—could have noticed anything wrong. There was nothing to wash out. There was no stain of any kind. There were no spots of blood anywhere. I had been too careful for that. A tub had caught all—ha! ha!

When I had finished all this work, it was four o'clock. It was still as dark as midnight. As the clock struck four, I heard a knocking at the street door. With a light heart, I went down to open it. The Evil Eye was gone. There was nothing now to fear. Three men entered the house. They introduced themselves as police officers. They said a scream had been heard by a neighbor during the night. Foul play was suspected. A report had been made at the police station. The police officers had been sent out to search the house.

I smiled—for what did I have to fear? I greeted the officers warmly. The scream, I said, was my own. I had had a bad dream. The old man, I said, was on vacation in the country. I took my visitors all over the house. I told them to search—search *well*. Finally, I took them to his room. I showed them his belongings, safe and undisturbed. Feeling very confident, I even brought chairs into the room. I told the officers to rest for a while. Quite sure of myself, I even put my own chair right over the old man's body.

The officers believed me. I was at ease. They sat there for a while, chatting about everyday things. But, before long, I felt myself getting pale. I wished they would go. My head ached, and I thought I heard a ringing in my ears. Yet still they sat and talked. The ringing in my ears became louder. I talked more to get rid of the feeling. But the noise kept getting louder. Finally, I realized that the noise was not within my ears.

I started to grow very pale. I began to talk even faster, and in a louder voice. Yet the sound got louder. What could I do? It was a low, dull, quick sound. It sounded like a watch wrapped in cotton. I gasped for breath. Still, the police officers did not hear it. I talked faster and louder, but the noise kept increasing. I stood up and moved around. I talked about things that were not important. I spoke in a high voice, and I used violent gestures—but the noise kept getting louder.

Why would they not be gone? I walked back and forth on the floor with heavy steps, but the noise kept getting louder. Oh, God! What *could* I do? The noise grew louder—louder—louder! And still the men chatted pleasantly and smiled. Was it possible that they didn't hear the sound? Almighty God! No, no! They heard! They suspected! They knew! They were making fun of me! This is what I thought, and it is what I still think.

But anything was better than this agony! Anything was better than to let them go on making a fool of me! I could look at their smiles no longer! I felt that I must scream or die! And now, again, listen! The sound is louder! *Louder!*

"Villains!" I screamed. "Pretend no more! I admit the deed! Tear up the floor boards! Here, here! It is the beating of his hideous heart!"

The Black Cat

Can addiction lead a good man into evil deeds? This story shows the gradual decay of a diseased mind. One step at a time, the main character sinks deeper and deeper into a hell of his own making. Read on for a chilling portrait of self-destruction.

AS I CAME CLOSER, I SAW THE FIGURE OF A GIANT CAT
ON THE WALL.

The Black Cat

I don't expect anyone to believe the fantastic story that I am about to tell. I would have to be mad to expect anyone to believe it. I hardly believe it myself— and I saw everything that happened. Yet, I am not mad—and I know that this is not a dream. Tomorrow I die. Today I wish to get this weight off my soul.

I want to place before the world a set of common, everyday events. I wish to do this in a plain and clear manner, without comment. These events have terrified me—have tortured me—have destroyed me. Yet I will not try to explain them. To

Edgar Allan Poe

me, they have caused only horror. After I die, maybe someone will be able to find a reason for everything that happened. Or maybe someone else will see that the events were nothing more than a set of natural causes and effects.

Ever since I was a baby, I have been known for being sweet and kind. In fact, my friends would make fun of me for this. I was especially fond of animals, and my parents let me have many pets. I spent most of my time with these pets. The only time I was really happy was when I was feeding and playing with them.

This quality in my character grew stronger as I grew older. By the time I was a man, my love of pets was one of my main sources of pleasure. I don't have to explain this to anyone who has loved a faithful and wise dog. There is something in the unselfish love of an animal that goes directly to one's heart.

I married early and was happy to discover that my wife had attitudes that were similar to mine. When she saw how much I enjoyed pets, she got many of the best kinds. We had birds, goldfish, a fine dog, rabbits, a small monkey, and a cat.

This cat was a remarkably large and beautiful animal. It was entirely black, and extremely wise. My wife was the first to notice how intelligent the cat was. Being a little superstitious, she told me the old folk tale about black cats really being witches in disguise. Of course, she wasn't really serious about this. I only mention it now because I just happened to remember it.

The cat's name was Pluto. He was my favorite pet and playmate. I alone fed him, and he followed me wherever I went in the house. He even tried to follow me when I went out into the streets.

Our friendship lasted, in this manner, for several years. During these years, my general attitude and character became much worse. This happened because I had started drinking too much. Each day, I became harder to get along with. I didn't care about anyone else's feelings. I even used bad language to my wife.

Finally, I became violent with her.

My pets, of course, also suffered. I not only neglected them, but I also mistreated them. I still had enough feeling for Pluto, however, that I didn't hurt him. But I didn't care if I mistreated the rabbits, the monkey, or even the dog, if they got in my way. Still my disease grew—and what disease is as bad as alcohol! Finally, I even started to mistreat Pluto, who was getting old by now.

One night, I came home drunk and imagined that the cat was avoiding me. When I seized him, he became frightened at my violence. The cat bit my hand, leaving a slight wound. I was so angry that I hardly even recognized myself. It seemed that my original soul left my body and a terrible evil took over. I took a pocket knife from my vest and opened it. Then I held the poor animal by the throat and cut one of its eyes from the socket! I blush, I burn, I shudder just to remember this terrible deed.

Reason returned with the morning. I had slept off the fumes of the alcohol.

But now I had a feeling—half of horror and half of remorse—for what I had done. At most, it was a weak feeling. My soul remained untouched. Again, I started drinking. Soon all memory of the deed was drowned in wine.

In the meantime, the cat slowly got better. The socket of his lost eye looked frightening, but he didn't seem to be in pain. The cat went about the house as usual, but he ran away whenever I came near. Of course, he was terrified of me. At first, I felt sorrow about this dislike on the part of an animal that had once loved me. But my feeling of sorrow soon turned into a feeling of irritation. And then it began to turn into a spirit of evil.

The spirit of evil is not well understood. Yet I am sure that it leans heavily on all human hearts. It gives direction to the human character. Who has not done something evil or stupid—for no other reason than because he knows he should *not*? Don't we all have a desire to break rules simply because they are rules? This spirit of evil, I say, came to be my final downfall. It was this endless longing of the soul to *vex itself*—to do wrong simply for wrong's sake.

The evil feeling within made me want to injure the cat even more. One morning, in cold blood, I slipped a noose around the cat's neck. I hung it to the limb of a tree. I did this with tears streaming from my eyes. Even as I was doing it, I felt remorse in my heart. Yet I hung the cat *because* I knew that it had loved me. I did it *because* I felt it had given me no reason to hurt it. I did it *because* I knew that in so doing, I was committing a sin. I knew it was a deadly sin that would never be forgiven.

That night, I was awakened from sleep by the cry of fire. The curtains around my bed were in flames. The whole house was blazing! It was with great difficulty that my wife, a servant, and I got out of the house. Before the night was over, the whole house was burned. All my possessions were gone.

I fell into despair. I am not trying to say that what I did caused the fire in any way. No! I am just telling the things that happened, in the order in which they happened.

On the day after the fire, I visited the ruins of my home. All but one of the walls had fallen in. The wall that still stood had been in the middle of the house. The head of my bed had rested against this wall. I remembered that the wall had recently been replastered. I thought that maybe the fresh plaster was what had saved it.

A big crowd of people was gathered around the wall. I could hear some people saying, "Strange!" Others were saying, "Unusual!" As I came closer, I saw the figure of a giant cat on the wall. It looked as if it had been carved there. There was a rope around the animal's neck.

When I first saw this, I felt extreme terror. Then I remembered that the cat had been hung in a garden next to the house. When the fire started, a crowd of people had gathered in the garden. Someone must have seen the cat, cut it from the tree, and thrown it through my bedroom window. Perhaps they had done this to try to wake me up. The falling of the other walls may have pushed the cat into the fresh plaster. Then the fire itself had somehow produced this strange effect on the wall.

Even though I could explain what must have happened, it was still frightening. For months I could not forget the sight of the cat figure on the wall, I felt something like remorse—but it was not really remorse. I even began to miss the animal and started looking for another cat that looked like the beautiful, black Pluto.

One night when I was out in a bar, I noticed a black object in a corner of the room. I thought I knew what it was, so I went closer to see it better. It was a black cat—a very large one. It was as large as Pluto, and it was like him in every detail but one. Pluto didn't have a single white hair anywhere on his body. This cat had a large patch of white on his chest.

When I touched him, he jumped up. He purred loudly, rubbed against my hand, and seemed very happy. It seemed that this was the very cat I was looking for. I offered to buy it from the owner of the bar. But he claimed he had never seen the cat before.

I continued to pet the cat until I was ready to go home. As I started to leave, the cat showed that he wanted to go with me. I let him do so, bending down and petting him from time to time as we walked. When we got to my house, he seemed to fit right in. From the very beginning, he became a great favorite with my wife.

As for me, I soon found that I disliked the cat. This was just the opposite of what I had expected. I cannot explain how or why, but the cat's fondness for me made me disgusted and annoyed. Slowly these feelings changed into hatred. I avoided the animal. Only a sense of shame for what I had done to Pluto kept me from hurting the cat.

For many weeks I did not do anything to harm him. But slowly, very slowly, I began to look upon the cat with terrible hatred. If the cat came into a room, I would leave it, as if I were avoiding some terrible disease.

Perhaps I forgot to tell you about the strange thing I noticed the morning after I had brought the cat home. It was then that I saw that, like Pluto, he was missing one eye. This fact, however, only made my wife love him more.

The more I hated the cat, the more it seemed to love me. It followed me wherever I went. When I sat, it would crouch beneath my chair or jump up into my lap. If I got up to walk, it would get between my feet and almost trip me. Sometimes it would put its long and sharp claws into my clothing and climb, in this way, to my chest. At such times, I longed to destroy the cat with a single blow. Yet I stopped myself from doing it. For one thing, I was ashamed of what I had done to Pluto. But the real reason was that I was afraid of this cat.

It was not physical harm that I feared. Yet, I don't know how else to explain it. I am almost ashamed to admit it, even as I sit in my prison cell. The terror and horror that the cat made me feel was caused by the white hair on his chest. This white hair was the only difference between this cat and the one I had destroyed.

When I first got the cat, the form of this mark didn't look like anything special. But slowly, the shape became clearer and clearer. It now looked like an object that I shudder even to name. The white mark was in the shape of something terrible and frightening—the gallows! The place of hanging! Oh, terrible place of horror and of crime—of agony and of death!

Because of this frightening mark, I was now miserable beyond words. *If only I had dared*, I would have gotten rid of the cat. But alas. Neither by day nor by night did I know a moment of rest. During the day, the cat didn't leave me alone for a moment. During the night, I had frightening dreams that woke me every hour. Each time I woke up, I found the hot breath of the cat upon my face. It was then that I knew that the weight of the cat would always be upon my heart!

Now I began to have nothing but evil thoughts. I hated all things and all people. My poor wife suffered through my bad moods without complaining.

One day my wife joined me on a household errand. As we went to the cellar of the house, the cat followed us down the steep stairs. Slipping between my feet, he almost tripped me. This pushed me into madness, making me forget the fear that had stopped me until then.

Without thinking, I lifted up an axe and aimed a blow at the cat. This blow would have killed the cat immediately if it had fallen as I wished. But my wife stopped me before I could bring down my arm. Now I was pushed into an even greater rage. I pulled away from her grasp—and buried the axe in her brain! She fell dead upon the spot without even a groan.

I knew I had to do something to hide the body. I could not take it out of the house, either by day or by night. To do so would run the risk of being seen by the neighbors.

Other ideas came to me. One was to burn the body. Another was to dig a grave for it in the floor of the cellar. I also thought about throwing it down the well in the yard. I even thought about packing it in a box, as if it were merchandise of some kind. Then I could have a servant take it from the house. Finally I thought of walling it up in the cellar.

The cellar was well-suited for such a purpose. Its walls were loose and had recently been coated over with a rough plaster. The dampness of the air had kept the plaster from hardening. Also, one of the walls had a section that had originally been a fireplace. The fireplace had been walled over to look like the rest of the cellar. I knew it would be easy to remove the old bricks. Then I could put the body inside and wall the whole thing up again. No one would be able to tell the difference.

I used a crowbar to remove the bricks. Then I carefully put the body against the inner wall of the fireplace. It was a simple matter to put all the bricks back in place. Next I carefully spread new plaster over the bricks. When I was finished, I stepped back to look at what I had done. The wall looked perfect. No one would be able to tell it had been disturbed.

Then I looked around for the cat that had caused me so much trouble. I was now determined to put it to death. If I had seen it right then, there is no doubt about what I would have done. But the animal seemed to be hiding somewhere. It must have been frightened by the violence of my anger. I could not find it anywhere, and it did not show up during the night. So, for one night at least, I had a good night's sleep. It was my first peaceful night since the cat had come home with me that night.

The second and the third day passed, and still the cat did not appear. My happiness was supreme! The thought of what I had done to my wife disturbed me but little. Some people had asked about her, but I made up a story to explain her absence. A search had even been done, but of course nothing was found. Now I looked upon my future happiness as certain.

On the fourth day, the police came to the house again. They made another search of our apartment—this time including the grounds and the cellar. They left no corner untouched. Finally, they went down to the cellar for the last time. I wasn't even nervous. My heart beat as calmly as if I were sleeping and having pleasant dreams. I walked back and forth in the cellar, holding my folded arms across my chest. I strolled to and fro. The police were finally beginning to get ready to go.

As they were leaving, I started talking to them. The happiness I felt in my heart was far too strong to be held in. "Gentlemen," I said, as they were climbing up the steps, "I am so glad that I was able to be of help. I wish you all good health. By the way, gentlemen, this is a very well-built house. Don't you agree?" (I don't know why I kept on talking. It seemed as if I couldn't help myself.) "These walls are very solid," I said. I was holding a cane in my hand, which I used to rap on the wall. I rapped on that very part of the wall that hid my wife's body!

As soon as the noise of my rapping had faded into silence, a voice was heard from within the tomb! It was a cry—at first soft and low, like the sobbing of a child. But it quickly became one long, loud, and continuous scream. The cry didn't sound human. It was a howl, a wailing shriek, half of horror and half of triumph.

It is foolish to speak about what I was thinking. Almost fainting, I staggered to the opposite wall. For a moment the police stood still on the stairs, frozen in terror. In the next moment, a dozen strong arms were pulling at the wall. It fell easily. The body, already beginning to rot, lay there in front of the police. On its head, staring at us with its one eye, sat the hideous cat. It was the cat who had driven me to murder and then given me up to the hangman. I had walled the monster up within the tomb.

Thinking About
the Stories

The Cask of Amontillado

1. Story ideas come from many sources. Do you think this story is drawn more from the author's imagination or from real-life experience? What clues in the "About the Author" section might support your opinion?

2. Did the story plot change direction at any point? Explain the turning point of the story.

3. Suppose this story had a completely different outcome. Can you think of another effective ending for this story?

The Masque of the Red Death

1. All stories fit into one or more categories. Is this story serious or funny? Would you call it an adventure, a love story, or a

mystery? Is it a character study? Or is it simply a picture the author has painted of a certain time and place? Explain your thinking.

2. Many stories are meant to teach a lesson of some kind. Is the author trying to make a point in this story? What is it?

3. Imagine that you have been asked to write a short review of this story. In one or two sentences, tell what the story is about and why someone would enjoy reading it.

The Tell-Tale Heart

1. What is the title of this story? Can you think of another good title?

2. The plot is the series of events that takes place in a story. Usually, story events are linked in some way. Can you name an event in this story that was the cause of a later event?

3. All the events in a story are arranged in a certain order, or sequence. Tell about one event from the beginning of this story, one from the middle, and one from the end. How are these events related?

The Black Cat

1. Look at the illustration that introduces this story. What character or characters are pictured? What is happening in the scene? What clues does the picture give you about the time and place of the story?

2. Good writing always has an effect on the reader. How did you feel when you finished reading this story? Were you surprised, horrified, amused, sad, touched, or inspired? What elements in the story made you feel that way?

3. Some stories are packed with action. In other stories, the key events take place in the minds of the characters. Is this story told more through the characters' thoughts and feelings? Or is it told more through their outward actions?